SHARK ATTACK!

by Julia March

Editor Rosie Peet
Designer Jon Hall
Senior Editor Emma Grange
Pre-production Producer Rebecca Fallowfield
Producer Louise Daly
Managing Editor Paula Regan
Design Manager Jo Connor
Publisher Julie Ferris
Art Director Lisa Lanzarini
Publishing Director Simon Beecroft

Cover designed by Sam Bartlett

First American Edition, 2017
Published in the United States by DK Publishing
345 Hudson Street, New York, New York 10014

Page design copyright © 2017 Dorling Kindersley Limited
DK, a Division of Penguin Random House LLC
16 17 18 19 10 9 8 7 6 5 4 3 2 1
001–299082–Aug/2017

A catalog record for this book is available from the Library of Congress.

ISBN: 978-1-4654-6193-3 (Paperback)
ISBN: 978-1-4654-6194-0 (Hardback)

DK books are available at special discounts when
purchased in bulk for sales promotions, premiums,
fund-raising, or educational use. For details, contact:
DK Publishing SpecialMarkets,
345 Hudson Street, New York, New York 10014
SpecialSales@dk.com

Printed and bound in China

A WORLD OF IDEAS:
SEE ALL THERE IS TO KNOW

www.dk.com
www.LEGO.com

Contents

Ninjago® City

Welcome to Ninjago® City.
This busy city is home to
thousands of people.

Six brave ninja live in
Ninjago City.
Their job is to defend the
city from dangers of all kinds.

Ninja defenders

An evil villain keeps attacking
the peaceful city.
The people who live here have
to rebuild it again and again.

The ninja want to stop
the villain once and for all.
Next time he comes,
they will be ready.

Lord Garmadon

Meet Lord Garmadon.
He is the evil villain who keeps
destroying Ninjago City.
Garmadon wears a big
helmet with horns.
He has four arms.
Just look at his mean red eyes!

Shark Army

Garmadon plans to invade
Ninjago City again.
This time he will bring his
Shark Army.

His shark soldiers look like
sea creatures.
They are armed with fishy
weapons and vehicles.

Shark-Army vehicles

Here are some of the Shark Army's battle vehicles. If you see them coming... run!

Flying Jelly Sub

Beware of the Jelly Sub's toxic tentacles.

Manta Ray Bomber

Look out!
The Manta Ray is
ready to drop its bombs.

Crab Mech

Avoid the
Crab Mech's
snapping claws.

Volcano hideout

Garmadon's hideout is inside a big, hot volcano. Garmadon often gets angry with his generals. When he does, he fires them out of the volcano. This general has been fired. His clothes are ruined!

Brand-new mech

Garmadon's scientists have built him a Shark Mech. Garmadon cackles with delight. He plans to stomp into the city in the Shark Mech. He will show those ninja who is boss!

Shark Mech

In his Shark Mech, Garmadon can chase his foes anywhere. It can walk under water, on land, and even up walls!

Huge hand can grab enemies

Feet have suction cups to walk up walls

Garmadon sits in this cockpit

Gun fires out live sharks

Mech battle

Here comes Lord Garmadon
with his Shark Army.
He gets a big surprise.
The ninja have mechs too!

The ninja chase the villains
out of Ninjago City.
Good job, ninja!

Quiz

1. How many ninja live in Ninjago City?

2. What do Shark Army soldiers look like?

3. What color are Lord Garmadon's eyes?

4. Who built the Shark Mech?

5. Where is Lord Garmadon's hideout?

Index

4. Garmadon's scientists 5. Inside a volcano
1. Six 2. Sea creatures 3. Red
Quiz Answers

A Note to Parents

THIS BOOK is part of an exciting four-level reading series
for children, developing the habit of reading widely for
both pleasure and information.

Beautiful illustrations and superb full-color images combine with
engaging, easy-to-read narratives to offer a fresh approach to each
subject in the series. Each book is guaranteed to capture a child's
interest while developing his or her reading skills, general
knowledge, and love of reading.

The four levels of reading books are aimed at different reading
abilities, enabling you to choose the books that are exactly right for
your child:

Level 1: Learning to read
Level 2: Beginning to read
Level 3: Beginning to read alone
Level 4: Reading alone

The "normal" age at which a child begins to read can be anywhere
from three to eight years old. Adult participation through the lower
levels is very helpful for providing encouragement, discussing
storylines, and sounding out unfamiliar words.

No matter which level you
select, you can be sure that
you are helping your child learn
to read, then read to learn!